Manuel de
FALLA

THE THREE CORNERED HAT

Scenes and Dances from Part 1

Edited by
Clinton F. Nieweg
Julia L. McAlister

Study Score
Partitur

SERENISSIMA MUSIC, INC.

ORCHESTRA

2 Flutes (2nd also Piccolo)
2 Oboes (2nd also English horn)
2 Clarinets (B-flat and A)
2 Bassoons

2 Horns (F)
2 Trumpets (C)

Timpani
Cymbals
Xylophone/Bells
Piano
Harp

Violin I
Violin II
Viola
Violoncello
Bass

Duration: ca. 14 minutes

First performance (complete ballet): July 22, 1919
London, Alhambra Theatre
Orchestra of the Ballets Russes
Ernest Ansermet, conductor

This study score is an unabridged licensed reprint – in reduced format – of the large
conductor's score first issued by Kalmus. The large score and a complete set of parts
are available for sale from the Kalmus catalog as number A 8293.

Edwin F. Kalmus, LC
P. O. Box 5011
Boca Raton, FL 33431-0811
Phone: 561-241-6340; 800-434-6340
Fax: 561-241-6347
Website: www.efkalmus.com

THE THREE-CORNERED HAT

Scenes and Dances from Part 1

MANUEL DE FALLA
Edited by Clinton F. Nieweg
and Julia L. McAlister

INTRODUCTION
Allegro ma non troppo ($\,\s"= 104$)

SERENISSIMA MUSIC, INC.

10
a 2
Hn.
f marcato
Tpt.
Timp.
1
Vn.
2
Va.
Vc.
D.B.
19
G.P.
Hn.
mf
Tpt.
mf
Timp.
sffz
G.P.
1
Vn.
2
Va.
Vc.
D.B.
attacca

29
AFTERNOON
Allegretto (𝅗𝅥. = 50)
Eng. Hn.
Cl.
Timp.
Harp
1.
pp
p
mf
sulla tavola
f
marc.
Vn.
1
2
Va.
Vc.
D.B.
pizz.
mf marc.
sul ponticello
div.
pp
pizz.
37
dim.
stacc.
(F♮ E♭)
(B♮)
arco
cresc.
pos. nat.
unis.

45
1. solo
tr
Fl.
p
f
f
13
p
Ob.
Eng. Hn.
1. solo
tr
Cl.
p
f
1.
Bsn.
pp
mf
Hn.
p
Tpt.
Timp.
Cym.
Xylo.
Bells
Piano
pp
mf
pp
stacc.
p
f
Harp
sempre stacc.
sulla tavola
mf
p
(B♭)
f
45
1
Vn.
2
pp
pizz.
mf
p
arco
p
pp
Va.
pizz.
mf
f
mf
p
arco
p
pp
Vc.
pizz.
p
f
mf
p
p
marc.
f
D.B.
p
marc.
f
p

51
Fl.
Ob.
Eng. Hn.
Cl.
Bsn.
Hn.
Tpt.
Timp.
Cym.
Xylo.
Bells
Piano
Harp
1
Vn.
2
Va.
Vc.
D.B.
13
f
p
mf
pp
1.
(B♮)
(E♮)
(E♭)
pizz.
arco
tr

58
64
Fl.
Ob.
Eng. Hn.
Cl.
13
f
poco
f
Bsn.
1.
p
mf
Hn.
Tpt.
Timp.
p
mf
p
Cym.
Xylo. Bells
Piano
Harp
(B♭)
(B♮)
mf
f
p
64
p
2 soli con sord. div.
altri
mf
(sempre senza sord.)
3 soli, div.
arco
Vn.
1
2
pizz.
pp
mf
f
p
mf
2 soli con sord. div., arco
Va.
1
2
div.
pizz.
pp
mf
f
p
mf
(sempre senza sord.)
2 soli, div.
arco
pizz.
pp
mf
f
p
1. solo arco
mf
Vc.
pp
mf
f
p
p
2 soli
D.B.
poco
mf
f
p
p

65
poco rall.
affrettando
a tempo
Fl.
Ob.
Eng. Hn.
Cl.
Bsn.
Hn.
Tpt.
Timp.
Cym.
Xylo.
Bells
Piano
Harp
(C♯)
(C♮)
2. mf
(2 unis.)
p cresc.
tutti, div.
unis.
2 soli
prima metà
tutti, div.
arco
unis., pizz.
1
Vn.
2
1
Va.
2
Vc.
D.B.

72
1. solo
76
poco rit.
Fl.
Fl. 2 take Picc.
Picc.
Ob.
Eng. Hn.
Cl.
1.
espress.
Bsn.
Hn.
1. solo
espress.
Tpt.
Timp.
Cym.
Xylo.
Bells
Piano
poco
2 Ped.
Ped.
Ped.
Harp
(B♭)
(B♮)
(C♯)
76
poco rit.
unis.
senza sord.
1
Vn.
2
pizz.
1a metà arco
senza sord.
pizz.
arco
Va.
pizz.
arco
pizz.
arco
Vc.
pizz.
arco
D.B.
marc.

79
a tempo
Calmo e pesante (♩ = 72)
Fl.
Picc.
Ob.
Eng. Hn.
Cl.
Bsn.
1. solo
marc. ma p
Hn.
Tpt.
Timp.
Cym.
Xylo.
Bells
Piano
Harp
Vn.
tutti
p cresc.
Va.
Vc.
1. solo pizz.
arco
D.B.

86
91
più mosso (♩= 112)
Fl.
Picc.
Ob.
Eng. Hn.
Cl.
Bsn.
sempre stacc.
f p
p subito
ff
1.
Hn.
Tpt.
Timp.
Cym.
Xylo.
Bells
Piano
p stacc.
Harp
mf stacc.
pizz.
1
Vn.
2
Va.
Vc.
D.B.
tutti, (sempre pizz.)
p subito

95
Fl.
Picc.
Ob.
mf cresc.
Eng. Hn.
Cl.
mf cresc.
Bsn.
mf cresc.
Hn.
mf
Tpt.
Timp.
Cym.
Xylo.
Bells
Piano
f
Harp
1
Vn.
2
mf cresc.
f
Va.
mf cresc.
f
Vc.
mf cresc.
f
D.B.
mf cresc.
f

104
Fl.
Picc.
Ob.
Eng. Hn.
Cl.
Bsn.
Hn.
Tpt.
Timp.
Cym.
Xylo.
Bells
Piano
Harp
1
Vn.
2
Va.
Vc.
D.B.
ff
a 2
f

112
114
pochissimo rit.
Fl.
Picc.
Ob.
Eng. Hn.
Cl.
Bsn.
Hn.
Tpt.
Timp.
Cym.
Xylo.
Bells
Piano
Harp
Vn.
Va.
Vc.
D.B.
a 2
1. solo
arco
pizz.
tr

DANCE OF THE MILLER'S WIFE (FANDANGO)

In all the bars marked ✻ the last two eighth notes must be very slightly held back.   41861

123
Fl.
Picc.
Ob.
Eng. Hn.
Cl.
Bsn.
Hn.
Tpt.
Timp.
Cym.
Xylo.
Bells
Piano
Harp
1
Vn.
2
Va.
Vc.
D.B.
cresc.
modo ord.
cresc.
modo ord.
cresc.
ff
p
f

126
129
*
Fl.
Picc.
Ob.
Eng. Hn.
Cl.
p stacc.
Bsn.
p
cresc.
f
Hn.
p
cresc.
Tpt.
Timp.
f
Cym.
Xylo.
Bells
Piano
p
Harp
1
Vn.
2
spiccato
cresc.
modo ord.
Va.
Vc.
pizz.
mf
D.B.
arco

130
Fl.
Picc.
Ob.
Eng. Hn.
Cl.
stacc.
Bsn.
Hn.
Tpt.
Timp.
Cym.
Xylo.
Bells
Piano
Harp
1
Vn.
2
Va.
Vc.
D.B.
pizz.
arco

135
137
Fl.
Picc.
Ob.
Eng. Hn.
Cl.
Bsn.
Hn.
Tpt.
Timp.
Cym.
Xylo.
Piano
Harp
Vn.
Va.
Vc.
D.B.
cresc.
f stacc.
1. solo, con sord.
Xylo.
pizz.
arco
ff
f
mf

139
Fl.
Picc.
Ob.
Eng. Hn.
Cl.
Bsn.
Hn.
Tpt.
Timp.
Cym.
Xylo.
Piano
Harp
1
Vn.
2
Va.
Vc.
D.B.
tr
ff
p
f
spiccato
modo ord.
pizz.
arco
mf
3

142
tr
Fl.
Picc.
Ob.
Eng. Hn.
Cl.
Bsn.
p
Hn.
p
Tpt.
3
Timp.
Cym.
Xylo.
Piano
Harp
1
Vn.
2
spiccato
p
Va.
spiccato
p
Vc.
pizz.
mf
D.B.

145
Fl.
Picc.
Ob.
Eng. Hn.
Cl.
Bsn.
Hn.
Tpt.
Timp.
Cym.
Xylo.
Piano
Harp
1
Vn.
2
Va.
Vc.
D.B.
più p
modo ord.
modo ord.
arco

148
pochissimo rit.
a tempo
Fl.
Picc.
Ob.
Eng. Hn.
Cl.
Bsn.
Hn.
Tpt.
Timp.
Cym.
Xylo.
Bells
Piano
Harp
colle bacchette
stacc.
148
pochissimo rit.
a tempo
1
Vn.
2
Va.
Vc.
D.B.
vibrando
stacc. molto
stacc. molto
stacc. molto
stacc. molto

151
Fl.
Picc.
Ob.
Eng. Hn.
Cl.
Bsn.
Hn.
Tpt.
Timp.
Cym.
Xylo.
Bells
Piano
Harp
1
Vn.
2
Va.
Vc.
D.B.
sffz
ff
stacc.
3
5

154
Fl.
Picc.
Ob.
Eng. Hn.
Cl.
Bsn.
Hn.
Tpt.
Timp.
Cym.
Xylo.
Bells
Piano
Harp
Vn.
1
2
Va.
Vc.
D.B.
sffz
stacc.
3
5
6
(G♮)
pizz.

158
Fl.
Picc.
Ob.
Eng. Hn.
Cl.
Bsn.
Hn.
Tpt.
B♭ to C
Timp.
Cym.
Xylo.
Bells
Piano
Harp
6
1
Vn.
2
Va.
Vc.
D.B.
sffz
tr
mf
p
f
spiccato
pizz.
arco

162
Fl.
Picc.
Ob.
Eng. Hn.
Cl.
Bsn.
Hn.
Tpt.
Timp.
Cym.
Xylo.
Bells
Piano
Harp
162
1
Vn.
2
Va.
Vc.
D.B.
f
sffz
stacc.
mf
ff
pos. nat.
arco

165
Fl.
Picc.
Ob.
Eng. Hn.
Cl.
Bsn.
Hn.
Tpt.
Timp.
Cym.
Xylo.
Bells
Piano
Harp
1
Vn.
2
Va.
Vc.
D.B.
sffz
ff
mf
take Oboe
stacc.
(F♮)

168
Fl.
Picc.
Ob.
Cl.
take A Clarinet
Bsn.
Hn.
Tpt.
Timp.
Cym.
Xylo.
Bells
Piano
Harp
(E♮ F♯ A♯)
1
Vn.
2
Va.
Vc.
D.B.
pizz.

171
Fl.
Picc.
Ob.
1. solo
mf marc.
Cl.
Bsn.
Hn.
Tpt.
Timp.
C to D
Cym.
Xylo.
Bells
Piano
Harp
gliss.
(E♮ F♯ A♯)
171
Vn.
sul tasto
Va.
sul tasto
Vc.
sul tasto
D.B.
div.
arco
(pizz.)

174
Fl.
Picc.
Ob.
Cl.
Bsn.
Hn.
Tpt.
Timp.
Cym.
Xylo.
Bells
Piano
Harp
C♯
A♮
1
Vn.
2
Va.
Vc.
D.B.
mf marc.
marc. ma p
pos. nat.
sul tasto
unis., pizz.
arco
div.
pizz.

177
179
Fl.
Picc.
1
Ob.
2
Cl.
in A
Bsn.
Hn.
(senza sord.)
Tpt.
Timp.
Cym.
Xylo.
Bells
Piano
Harp
(B♮ F♯)
179
Vn.
1
2
Va.
Vc.
D.B.
pos. nat.
div.
arco, unis.

180
Fl.
Picc.
1
Ob.
2
Cl.
Bsn.
Hn.
Tpt.
Timp.
Cym.
Xylo.
Bells
Piano
Harp
1
Vn.
2
Va.
Vc.
D.B.
sfz
mf
p
ff
tr

182
Fl.
Picc.
1
Ob.
2
Cl.
Bsn.
Hn.
Tpt.
Timp.
Cym.
Xylo.
Bells
Piano
Harp
1
Vn.
2
Va.
Vc.
D.B.
sfz
p cresc.
mf
cresc.
p
poco cresc.
ff
Ped.
tr

187
185
Fl.
Picc.
1
Ob.
2
Cl.
Bsn.
Hn.
Tpt.
Timp.
Cym.
Xylo.
Bells
Piano
Harp
1
Vn.
2
Va.
Vc.
D.B.
mf cresc.
f
ff
take Eng. Hn.
ff marc.
marc.
mf
Ped.
div.
cresc.
stacc. molto marc.
div., pizz.
pizz.
f marc.

188
Ob.
Cl.
Bsn.
Hn.
Timp.
Harp
Vn.
Va.
Vc.
D.B.
solo
marc.
2. take B♭ Cl.
(1a metà)
poco cresc.
p stacc. sempre
div.
192
Eng. Hn.
[mf] cresc. molto
f cresc.
(E♭ F♮ B♭)
dim.
poco cresc.

197
Ob.
Eng. Hn.
Cl.
in B♭
Bsn.
Hn.
Timp.
A to G
Harp
Vn.
Va.
Vc.
D.B.
poco cresc.
p sempre stacc.
cresc.
marc.
202
(A♭)
poco
dim.
p stacc. sempre
arco
(pizz.)

206
207
Fl.
Picc.
Ob.
Eng. Hn.
Cl.
2. in B♭
mf stacc.
Bsn.
Hn.
1. solo, con sord.
Tpt.
Timp.
Cym.
Xylo.
Piano
Harp
207
tutti
unis.
unis., arco
1
Vn.
2
Va.
Vc.
D.B.

209
211
Fl.
Picc.
Ob.
Eng. Hn.
1
Cl.
2
Bsn.
Hn.
Tpt.
Timp.
Cym.
Xylo.
Piano
Harp
1
Vn.
2
Va.
Vc.
D.B.
tr
fp
ff
p cresc.
mf
f
p
sf
spiccato
modo ord.
pizz.
cresc.
arco

212
Fl.
Picc.
Ob.
Eng. Hn.
1
Cl.
2
2. take A Cl.
Bsn.
p cresc.
Hn.
Tpt.
Timp.
p cresc.
Cym.
Xylo.
to Bells
Piano
Harp
spiccato
1
Vn.
2
spiccato
cresc.
Va.
Vc.
arco
pizz.
cresc.
D.B.

poco a poco affrettando
215
sempre affrettando poco a poco
Fl.
Picc.
Ob.
Eng. Hn.
molto
Cl.
take A Cl.
Bsn.
Hn.
Tpt.
Timp.
Cym.
Xylo.
Bells
Piano
Harp
215
poco a poco affrettando
sempre affrettando poco a poco
1
Vn.
2
modo ord.
modo ord.
cresc. molto
cresc. molto
Va.
cresc. molto
Vc.
arco
cresc. molto
D.B.

220
THE CORREGIDOR
Moderato
(♩ = 54)
1. solo
Bsn.
marc. ma non troppo forte
giusto, senza rall.
1
Vn.
2
Va.
Vc.
D.B.
228
THE MILLER'S WIFE
poco più mosso
(♩ = 66)
p
2 soli
altri
pizz.
mf
233
pp
cresc.
mf
pp subito
arco

238
poco rit.
a tempo, ma libero
rit. a piacere
THE GRAPES
Vivo
(♩. = 56)
Fl.
Bsn.
Hn.
a 2
Harp
Vn. 1 2
Va.
Vc.
D.B.
tutti
pizz.
arco
243
1.
245
stacc. sulla tavola
con sord.
sul pont.

248
Fl.
Picc.
Ob.
Eng. Hn.
Cl.
1. in A
Bsn.
1.
Hn.
1
2
Tpt.
con sord.
Timp.
Cym.
Xylo.
Bells
Piano
Harp
sempre molto stacc.
Vn.
1
2
con sord.
arco
pos. nat.
Va.
Vc.
D.B.

253
Fl.
Picc.
Ob.
Eng. Hn.
Cl.
Bsn.
1
Hn.
2
Tpt.
Timp.
Cym.
Xylo.
Bells
Piano
Harp
1
Vn.
2
Va.
Vc.
D.B.
tr
1.
2. p
p
mf
f
ff
Ped.

258
261
Fl.
Picc.
Ob.
Eng. Hn.
Cl.
Bsn.
1
Hn.
2
Tpt.
Timp.
Cym.
Xylo.
Bells
Piano
Harp
261
1
Vn.
2
Va.
Vc.
D.B.

263
Fl.
Picc.
Ob.
Eng. Hn.
Cl.
Bsn.
Hn.
Tpt.
Timp.
Cym.
Xylo.
Bells
Piano
Harp
1
Vn.
2
Va.
Vc.
D.B.
solo
E to D
(C♮ D♮)

268
272
Fl.
dolce
Picc.
Ob.
Eng. Hn.
tr
Cl.
Bsn.
2.
1. solo
Hn.
1. solo
Tpt.
Timp.
Cym.
Xylo.
Bells
Piano
Harp
272
1
Vn.
2
Va.
1
Vc.
2
1. solo
arco
dolce
altri
tutti
pizz.
D.B.

273
Fl.
Picc.
Ob.
Eng. Hn.
Cl.
Bsn.
2. solo
Hn.
Tpt.
Timp.
Cym.
Xylo.
Bells
Piano
Harp
1
Vn.
2
Va.
Vc.
D.B.

278
Fl.
Picc.
Ob.
Bsn.
a 2
Harp
gliss.
Vn.
1
2
Va.
Vc.
D.B.
pizz.
arco
cresc.
282
Cl.
(2. in A)
(E♮ G♮ A♮)

286
289
Fl.
Picc.
Ob.
Eng. Hn.
Cl.
Bsn.
1
Hn.
2
Tpt.
Timp.
Cym.
Xylo.
Bells
Piano
Harp
1
Vn.
2
Va.
Vc.
D.B.
arco
tr
p
mf
f
Ped.
289

290
Fl.
Picc.
Ob.
Eng. Hn.
Cl.
Bsn.
1
Hn.
2
Tpt.
Timp.
Cym.
Xylo.
Bells
Piano
Harp
1
Vn.
2
Va.
Vc.
D.B.
solo
1.
(sempre con sord.)
p stacc.
mf stacc.
p cresc.
cresc. sempre
p cresc. sempre
mf cresc. sempre
più marc. sempre

295
Fl.
Picc.
Ob.
Eng. Hn.
Cl.
Bsn.
Hn.
Tpt.
Timp.
Cym.
Xylo.
Bells
Piano
Harp
Vn.
Va.
Vc.
D.B.
appena
mf cresc. sempre
più f
take Ob.
take B♭ Cl.
cresc.
sfz
ff
sf
mf
f

299
(♩ = ♩.)
poco meno vivo
Hn.
1
2
sf
sfz
ff
p
Vn.
Va.
Vc.
D.B.
(senza sord.)
pizz.
arco
arco (senza sord.)
gliss.
f
pp
mf
306
Mosso (♩ = 112)
spiccato, sempre pp

311
315
molto ritmico
Fl.
Picc.
Ob.
1.
f
1
Cl.
2
in B♭
f
Bsn.
1. solo
mf
2.
cresc.
f
a 2
Hn.
f marc.
Tpt.
Timp.
f
Cym.
Xylo.
Bells
Piano
f stacc.
Harp
ff stacc.
311
315
molto ritmico
1
Vn.
2
f
f
Va.
div., pizz.
ff
Vc.
pizz.
mf
p
mf
div.
ff
D.B.
pizz.
mf
ff

317
Fl.
Picc.
Ob.
in B♭
Cl.
Bsn.
Hn.
Tpt.
Timp.
Cym.
Bells
Piano
Harp
Vn.
Va.
Vc.
D.B.
ff
f
ff marc.

322
323
Fl.
Picc.
1 Ob. 2
1 Cl. 2
Bsn.
Hn.
Tpt.
Timp.
Cym.
Bells
Piano
Harp
1 Vn. 2
1 Va. 2
Vc.
D.B.
mf stacc. molto
(F♮ C♮)
pizz.
div.
unis.

329
Fl.
Picc.
1
Ob.
2
Cl.
Bsn.
Hn.
Tpt.
Timp.
Cym.
Xylo.
Bells
Piano
Harp
1
Vn.
2
1
Va.
2
Vc.
D.B.
mf stacc. molto
stacc. molto
a 2
mf stacc.
mf sempre stacc.
arco
1.

336
337
Fl.
Picc.
Ob.
Cl.
Bsn.
Hn.
Tpt.
Timp.
Cym.
Xylo.
Bells
Piano
Harp
Vn.
1
2
Va.
1
2
Vc.
D.B.
ff
f
sf
sfz
molto dim.
a 2
molto stacc.
e dim.
unis., pizz.
arco

342
Fl.
Picc.
Ob.
Cl.
Bsn.
Hn.
Tpt.
Timp.
Cym.
Bells
Piano
Harp
Vn. 1
Vn. 2
Va. 1
Va. 2
Vc.
D.B.
ff
p
p cresc.
a 2
1.
f
ff marc.
mf cresc.
p cresc. sempre
mf cresc.
(div.)
pizz.

349
353
Fl.
Picc.
Ob.
a 2
ff
Cl.
f
Bsn.
f
a 2
f
Hn.
ff p
molto
fff
a 2
f
Tpt.
con sord.
fp
molto
ff
Timp.
f
f
Cym.
Xylo.
Bells
Piano
ff
Harp
ff
349
353
arco
1
Vn.
2
unis., pizz.
f
arco
ff p
molto
fff
non legato
ff p
molto
fff
non legato
Va.
unis.
arco
f
ff p
molto
fff
non legato
Vc.
(unis.)
arco
f
ff p
molto
fff
non legato
D.B.
arco
f
ff

357
tr
Fl.
ff
Picc.
f
Ob.
fff
Cl.
fff
1.
Bsn.
sf
ff
1
Hn.
2
(sempre con sord.)
Tpt.
mf
Timp.
f
Cym.
Xylo.
Bells
Piano
ff
senza pedale
Harp
ff sempre
357
pizz.
f marc.
arco
1
Vn.
2
Va.
Vc.
D.B.

364
365
Fl.
Picc.
Ob.
Cl.
Bsn.
ff pp
1
Hn.
2
Tpt.
1. solo
p
Timp.
B, D
Cym.
Xylo.
Bells
Piano
Harp
8va
f
365
1
Vn.
2
div., sul pont.
f pp
1
Va.
2
Vc.
p
ff pp
f
D.B.
pizz.
p
ff pizz.
f

373
pochissimo rit.
Fl.
Picc.
1
Ob.
2
Cl.
a 2
Bsn.
Hn.
senza sord.
Tpt.
Timp.
Cym.
Xylo.
Bells
Piano
gliss.
Harp
(D♮ E♮ F♯ A♮ B♮ C)
373
pochissimo rit.
tutti
pos. nat.
pizz.
arco
1
Vn.
2
unis.
Va.
Vc.
arco
D.B.

376
a tempo
Fl.
Picc.
take Flute
1
Ob.
2
Cl.
2.
Bsn.
Hn.
Tpt.
Timp.
Cym.
Xylo.
Bells
Piano
Harp
senza arpegg.
(B♮)
376
a tempo
1
Vn.
2
spiccato
Va.
spiccato
Vc.
pizz.
D.B.

380
Fl.
Ob.
1
Cl.
2
Bsn.
Hn.
Tpt.
con sord.
D to E
Timp.
Cym.
Xylo.
Bells
Piano
Harp
380
1
Vn.
2
Va.
Vc.
D.B.
spiccato
modo ord.
pizz.
arco
mf cresc.

384
Fl.
Ob.
1
Cl.
2
Bsn.
Hn.
Tpt.
Timp.
Cym.
Xylo.
Bells
Piano
Harp
384
1
Vn.
2
Va.
Vc.
D.B.
f
ff
staccato
p
mf
stacc.
modo ord.
pizz.
arco

388
Fl.
Ob.
1
Cl.
2
Bsn.
Hn.
Tpt.
Timp.
Cym.
Xylo.
Bells
Piano
Harp
1
Vn.
2
Va.
Vc.
D.B.
arco
arco
arco
f
ff
f > p

391
Fl.
Ob.
Cl.
Bsn.
Hn.
Tpt.
Timp.
Cym.
Xylo.
Bells
Piano
Harp
Vn.
Va.
Vc.
D.B.
2. take Picc.
E to D
gliss.
pizz.
arco

395
Fl.
Picc.
1
Ob.
2
Cl.
Bsn.
Hn.
Tpt.
Timp.
Cym.
Xylo.
Bells
Piano
Harp
1
Vn.
2
Va.
Vc.
D.B.
f
poco cresc.
mf
p
(B♭ C♯)
pizz.
spiccato
arco
spiccato
pp
poco
tr

399
Fl.
Picc.
Ob.
1.
Cl.
stacc. molto
Bsn.
Hn.
Tpt.
B to A
Timp.
Cym.
Xylo.
Bells
Piano
6
Harp
gliss.
(C♮)
1
Vn.
2
modo ord.
div.
Va.
arco
unis.
pizz.
Vc.
D.B.

403
404
Fl.
Picc.
Ob.
Cl.
Bsn.
Hn.
Tpt.
Timp.
Cym.
Xylo.
Bells
Piano
Harp
Vn.
Va.
Vc.
D.B.
2.
marc.
1. marc.
f
p
1.
marc.
sempre sord.
mf
f marc.
(F♯)
sempre 1a metà sola
tr
pp
10
marc., staccato
arco
div.

408
412
Fl.
Picc.
Ob.
Cl.
Bsn.
Hn.
Tpt.
Timp.
Cym.
Xylo.
Bells
Piano
Harp
Vn.
Va.
Vc.
D.B.
a 2
[mf] cresc. molto
p stacc.
cresc. molto
p stacc.
cresc.
A to G
tutti
pp sempre stacc.
p cresc.
sempre stacc.

413
Fl.
Picc.
Ob.
1. solo
a 2
Cl.
Bsn.
Hn.
f cresc.
Tpt.
1.
Timp.
Cym.
Xylo.
Bells
Piano
Harp
(E♭ B♭)
1
Vn.
2
Va.
Vc.
D.B.

418
Fl.
Picc.
Ob.
Cl.
Bsn.
Hn.
Tpt.
Timp.
Cym.
Xylo.
Bells
Piano
Harp
(A♭)
1
Vn.
2
Va.
Vc.
D.B.
mf
f cresc.
p
tr

422
Fl.
Picc.
Ob.
3
5
cresc.
Cl.
5
cresc.
Bsn.
mf
mf
1.
Hn.
p
Tpt.
Timp.
mf
Cym.
Xylo.
Bells
Piano
Harp
f
sempre prima metà
p
tr
tr
1
Vn.
2
mf
mf
p
cresc.
Va.
Vc.
unis., arco
D.B.
p stacc.
[mf
p]

426
animando, ma gradualmente sino al fine
Fl.
Picc.
Ob.
1
Cl.
2
Bsn.
Hn.
Tpt.
senza sord.
Timp.
Cym.
Xylo.
Bells
Piano
Harp
(B♮)
426
animando, ma gradualmente sino al fine
tutti
1
Vn.
2
Va.
Vc.
D.B.

430
Fl.
Picc.
Ob.
Cl.
a 2
Bsn.
Hn.
Tpt.
Timp.
Cym.
Xylo.
Bells
Piano
Harp
1
Vn.
2
Va.
Vc.
D.B.
pizz.
arco
cresc.

434
Fl.
Picc.
Ob.
Cl.
Bsn.
Hn.
Tpt.
f cresc.
Timp.
Cym.
Xylo.
Bells
Piano
6
6
Harp
1
Vn.
2
Va.
Vc.
D.B.

438
Fl.
Picc.
Ob.
Cl.
Bsn.
Hn.
Tpt.
Timp.
Cym.
Xylo.
Bells
Piano
Harp
1
Vn.
2
Va.
Vc.
D.B.
ff
sffz
a 2
8va